Ice Age
MAMMOTH

WILL THIS ANCIENT GIANT COME BACK TO LIFE?

By Barbara Hehner / Illustrations by Mark Hallett

Scientific consultation by Dr. Mark Engstrom and Dr. Kevin Seymour

A MADISON PRESS BOOK

produced for

CROWN PUBLISHERS ♕ NEW YORK

FROZEN IN TIME

*The trumpeting cries of a woolly mammoth
in distress blasted into the cold air of the Siberian
grasslands. Its mighty struggles only pulled it deeper into
the pool of soft mud in which it had fallen. A few
other mammoths, sensing danger, helplessly watched
from the boggy edge of the pool. Gradually, the grunts
and moans became fainter and then stopped.*

What killed this particular male mammoth in the prime of life over 20,000 years ago? Although scientists think that he stumbled into a mud pit, was trapped, and died there, they are not entirely certain what killed him. Did he suffocate in the mud? Did he die of starvation or of disease? Did he succumb to arrow wounds from a human hunter?

However the mammoth died, his body froze quickly and was buried in the permafrost — the layer of frozen ground found in northern regions that never thaws, even in summer. There he lay in his icy tomb while all recorded human history went by, from the building of the pyramids to the launching of the space shuttle.

In 1997, the mammoth's tusks, jutting from the ground, were discovered by Dolgan reindeer herders. They showed the tusks to a French

(Opposite) A mammoth struggles to escape from a mud-filled pit. Was this the Jarkov Mammoth 20,000 years ago? (Above) Bernard Buigues stands near the tusks of the Jarkov Mammoth, found in Siberia in 1997.

explorer named Bernard Buigues, who had been searching for many years for a well-preserved mammoth body. With the help of the Dolgan, Buigues organized an international expedition to unearth the Jarkov Mammoth, named for the family that found it.

In the fall of 1999, with fierce winter winds already raging in Siberia, the expedition team struggled to excavate the carcass. They knew that in the past, all mammoth remains had started to decay as soon as they began to thaw. Their goal was to keep this prehistoric treasure frozen until the team's scientists could examine it. If they could do that, they might be able to solve many mysteries about these long-dead animals and their way of life.

THE REINDEER PEOPLE

The Dolgan are one of the native peoples of northern Siberia. Even though many Dolgan now travel across the tundra in snowmobiles, they still use domesticated reindeer to pull their sleds and their *balloks*, which are portable homes on runners. They follow the migrating herds of wild reindeer, hunting them for food and for furs to make warm clothing. The Dolgan never shoot or eat their domesticated reindeer, which are given names and are carefully watched over — they are too valuable. The other thing of great value in the bleak landscape of northern Siberia is mammoth tusks. The Dolgan use them to make tools, reindeer harnesses, and buttons, but they also sell the tusks. Mammoth ivory is greatly prized by carvers, especially now that it is illegal to buy and sell elephant ivory. With the money they receive for the tusks, the Dolgan can buy medicine and kerosene.

UNEARTHING THE GIANT

Shuddering and swaying, one of Russia's largest helicopters strained to lift its massive cargo into the air. Over a period of several weeks, the expedition team had used pickaxes, shovels, and jackhammers to carve out a 23-ton (21,000 kg) block of rock-hard permafrost. But the mammoth was still out of sight, encased in the frozen earth. The team had then built a supporting iron framework around the block and attached industrial-strength cables to it. As the icebound mammoth swung and spun in its harness, the helicopter carried it almost 185 miles (300 km) west to the town of Khatanga.

Near Khatanga was a huge man-made cave that had been dug out of a hillside about 60 years earlier, for reasons no one could now remember. Windowless and so cold that the walls and floor glistened with a thick coat of ice, the cave was normally used for preserving frozen fish and reindeer carcasses. It was an uncomfortable place for scientists to work but it made an ideal storage room for the frozen mammoth.

In the fall of 2000, the scientists were ready to start their work on the mammoth remains using some surprising equipment — ordinary hair dryers! Bundled up in parkas to protect them from the frigid cold inside the cave, they stood on catwalks and pointed the dryers only at the parts they wanted to study. At this rate, it would probably take a full year to defrost all the sections they wanted to examine. As they thawed some patches of its three-foot-long (90-cm-long) hairs, they could already smell the mammoth's strong odor — not a decaying smell, just an earthy animal one. Working slowly and patiently, they also looked for ancient plants, pollen, and insects that might be caught in the mammoth's coat. For the first time in over 20,000 years, the skin, vertebrae, and ribs of the deep-frozen mammoth were again being exposed to the air.

Bernard Buigues examines the tusks of the Jarkov Mammoth.
(Above) The frozen mammoth is airlifted by helicopter to the Khatanga ice cave.

WHAT CAN WE LEARN FROM THE JARKOV MAMMOTH?

For the first time, scientists had an adult mammoth body to study in ideal laboratory conditions.

Blood — The mammoth may yield some of the oldest and best-preserved blood cells ever seen.

Bones — Along with the tissue and organs, the mammoth's bones could provide genetic material including possible DNA samples.

Hair — Were there different types of hair on different parts of its body, as with reindeer? Did its coat change with the seasons?

Heart, arteries, and internal organs — Tissue samples can give insight into how the mammoth lived and the state of its health.

Stomach — What were the contents of its last meal? Did it eat a broad range of plants or (as some scientists have suggested) did it depend on only a few types? Is there evidence of parasites?

Teeth and Tusks — The teeth revealed the mammoth was 47 years old. The outsides of the tusks were worn flat as the mammoth used its tusks to forage for grass. Some scientists have suggested mammoths used their tusks to chip away icicles on rocks and in crevices to get water to drink.

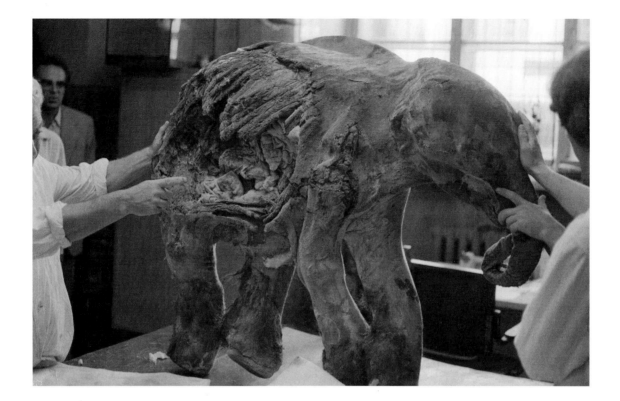

THE DISCOVERY OF DIMA, THE BABY MAMMOTH

Before the Jarkov expedition, the world's most famous mammoth was Dima, whose frozen carcass was uncovered by Siberian gold miners in 1977. Dima probably drowned in the icy waters of a steep-banked pond about 40,000 years ago. This makes him about twice as old as the Jarkov Mammoth. But he was also far younger — a baby less than a year old and just over three feet (90 cm) tall. His trunk was only two feet (60 cm) long and his tusks had not yet emerged.

Scientists discovered that the young mammoth had been thin and sickly even before his fatal accident. He had no food in his stomach and his body was infested with parasites. But Dima had more to tell researchers than his own tragic tale. He was one of the first mammoths to be carefully studied by an international team (above). For instance, Japanese scientists performed a CAT scan of Dima's organs and created a 3-D computer model of his heart. Dima's blood cells were still intact. By comparing a dried sample of his blood with elephant blood, American scientists were able to prove that mammoths were more closely related to Asian elephants than to African elephants. Dima's preserved carcass (right) is on display at the Russian Academy of Science's Zoological Museum in St. Petersburg.

AN AGE-OLD FASCINATION

Dinosaurs were extinct for more than 60 million years before our earliest ancestors appeared. But mammoths and early human beings existed at the same time. People who lived over 20,000 years ago in what is now France and Spain depicted woolly mammoths in large wall carvings and vivid black and red cave paintings. Their art is full of details that show just how well they knew these creatures: little eyes and

(Top) Cave artists at work. (Above) This reconstruction of a 20,000-year-old mammoth-bone hut is in Mezhirich, Ukraine. (Opposite) An ancient mammoth-ivory carving of a woman's head from France.

domed, tufted heads, and even the two "fingers" on the ends of mammoth trunks.

Some ancient peoples structured their lives around the mammoth, in much the same way that Native Americans of the plains later depended on the buffalo. Mammoths were more than just a source of food and clothing. All across Asia and in parts of Europe, paleontologists have found a fascinating array of tools and treasures made of mammoth bones and tusks. They have uncovered cleavers made from shoulder bones, anvils made from foot bones, and spears and boomerangs carved from mammoth tusks.

About 10,000 years ago, full-sized mammoths died out, and human memory of the massive creatures eventually faded and disappeared. But the bones — and even the frozen carcasses — of these animals remained in the ground. When a sudden thaw or a landslide uncovered some of these, later human beings were awestruck and struggled to account for what they saw. In Siberia, where decaying mammoth remains were often found, people believed they belonged to sinister giant rats that lived underground. It was supposed that if these animals came to the surface and were touched by the sun, they died. In many other places where mammoth bones were discovered, from England to North America, they were thought to belong to giant human beings who had once walked the earth.

By the seventeenth century, people who studied science began to look at mammoth finds more carefully. Most realized that the animals must have resembled elephants. But it took much longer for educated people to accept that these bones and tusks belonged to an animal that no longer existed. In the nineteenth century, it was a new idea, frightening to many, that animals could evolve (change) over time and that some could become extinct.

Today, our fascination with mammoths continues. Scientists have moved from studying the bones and hides of these animals to peering right into their body cells.

MAMMOTH ARTIFACTS

For thousands of years, craftsmen have used mammoth ivory to make beautiful ornaments and figurines. Although the mammoth's enormous tusks were hard and unyielding, ancient artisans discovered how to carve them using tools such as stone axes and bone chisels. By whittling, cutting, engraving, and scraping the ivory, the craftsmen created intricate shapes and designs. For some objects, the ivory may have been softened by soaking it in water or urine for several days before being heated over fire. Today, mammoth tusks are used by modern carvers, who continue to produce finely detailed objects like the examples shown above and below.

OUT OF AFRICA

Thrashing its way through the weed-choked pond, a piglike creature named *Moeritherium* scooped water plants into its mouth. This early ancestor of the mammoth lived about 50 million years ago in what is now northern Africa. *Moeritherium* weighed about 450 pounds (200 kg), with a thick neck and short, powerful legs. Its upper lip was long and flexible — not yet a trunk, but perhaps a beginning. It also had two jutting front teeth.

Moeritherium was the earliest known *proboscidean* — a group of mammals that would one day include mammoths, mastodons, and elephants. (The name comes from the Greek word *proboskis,* referring to their trunks.) Over the next 25 million years, *Moeritherium*'s descendants became bigger and bigger. The hoselike extensions of their noses and upper lips became longer, and their jutting incisors (cutting teeth) extended to form tusks. At the same time, the proboscideans lumbered out of Africa into Europe and Asia.

In a prehistoric pond, four of the mammoth's ancient proboscidean relatives dredge up vegetation while egrets search for fish the giants might disturb. (Far right) A huge, shovel-tusked Platybelodon.

About 25 million years ago, proboscideans had reached the general size and shape of elephants, with bulky bodies, legs like pillars, and muscular trunks. But as they spread through the world, their tusks and jaws continued to evolve in different species in strange and surprising ways. For instance, *Deinotherium,* the "hoe-tusker," had two tusks in its lower jaw that pointed down and curved back toward its body. Scientists think it might have used these tusks to rip bark off trees. *Gomphotherium* sported four tusks: two in the upper jaw that curved down, and two in the lower jaw that curved up. *Platybelodon,* one of the "shovel-tuskers," also had four tusks. However, the two in the upper jaw were short and straight, while the two in the lower jaw were flat and close together, forming a big scoop. *Platybelodon* probably used this scoop to dig up water plants.

The first true elephants appeared in Africa some 6 million years ago. About a million years later, the elephants split into three groups. One group stayed in Africa and became the ancestors of modern African elephants. Another group moved into Asia and gradually developed into modern Asian elephants. The third group became the mammoths. Mammoths are not the ancestors of modern elephants, as many people believe, but "cousins" who first appeared in the world at the same time. They first arrived in Europe about 2.5 million years ago. Shaggy coats were far in the future: these early mammoths still looked a lot like the elephant relatives they had left behind in Africa.

THE LAST OF THEIR KIND

Every part of the earth except Australia and Antarctica was once home to at least 300 different kinds of proboscideans. Of this great and varied tribe of tusks and trunks, only two types exist today. They are the African elephant (*Loxodonta africana*) and the Asian elephant (*Elephas maximus*). African elephants are the largest of all living land animals. The biggest stand 13 feet (4 m) tall at the shoulders and weigh 16,500 pounds (7,500 kg). Asian elephants are somewhat smaller, standing 10 feet (3 m) tall at the shoulders and weighing 11,000 pounds (5,000 kg) — about the same size as a woolly mammoth.

Besides the difference in their size, African and Asian elephants are quite easy to tell apart. African elephants have flat foreheads and large, fan-shaped ears that can be up to five feet (1.5 m) long. Asian elephants have dome-shaped heads and much smaller ear flaps — again, more like those of the woolly mammoth.

At the beginning of the twentieth century, about 2 million elephants thundered across the plains of central Africa; today, only 600,000 remain in the wild. Hunters have slaughtered thousands of them, mainly for the ivory in their tusks. Although the selling of ivory is now banned by most countries, it continues illegally. The Asian elephant is even more endangered — only 40,000 are now left in the wild. In both Asia and Africa, elephants are being crowded out as farmland and other developed areas take over their habitat.

MAMMOTH ANCESTORS AND RELATIONS

↑**CUVIERONIUS** (top)
South American Andean Mastodon
4.5 million – 10,000 years ago

↑**MAMMUT AMERICANUM**
American Mastodon
3.5 million – 10,000 years ago

MASTODONS & MAMMOTHS: WHAT'S THE DIFFERENCE?

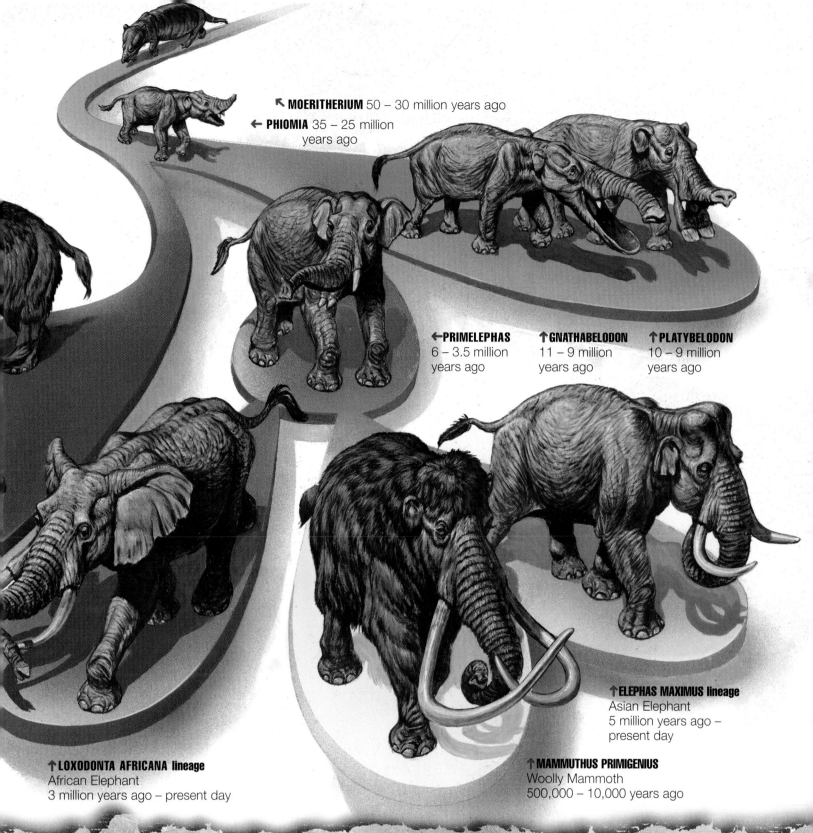

MOERITHERIUM 50 – 30 million years ago

PHIOMIA 35 – 25 million years ago

PRIMELEPHAS 6 – 3.5 million years ago

GNATHABELODON 11 – 9 million years ago

PLATYBELODON 10 – 9 million years ago

ELEPHAS MAXIMUS lineage Asian Elephant 5 million years ago – present day

LOXODONTA AFRICANA lineage African Elephant 3 million years ago – present day

MAMMUTHUS PRIMIGENIUS Woolly Mammoth 500,000 – 10,000 years ago

Mastodons and mammoths once lived together in North America but were very distinct animals. Mastodons were smaller, with flatter skulls, longer jaws, and tusks that were shorter and less curved. They had longer, stockier bodies and straighter backs. Mastodons also had a much older history, arriving in North America from Europe and Asia about 15 million years ago — long before mammoths even existed. Evolving into furry-coated American mastodons, they lived in forested areas and ate twigs and brush. Mammoths — which preferred open grasslands — didn't enter North America until about 1.5 million years ago and later evolved into the towering Columbian mammoth, which had a sparse coat. The shaggy woolly mammoth made the journey to North America only about 100,000 years ago — the day before yesterday to paleontologists!

THE BIG CHILL

The earth has gone through many great changes in its climate during its 4.6 billion years of existence. For long periods of time, it was much warmer than it is today, with no ice at all, even at the poles. At other times, ice covered up to a third of the earth. The colder periods are known as *ice ages*. Even during an ice age, there are milder times when the ice sheets retreat. The most recent ice age began about 1.7 million years ago and ended about 10,000 years ago. This time is also known as the *Pleistocene Epoch*. At its height, about 20,000 years ago, ice covered much of Europe, Asia, and North America. In North America, the ice reached as far south as present-day Missouri.

Farthest extent of ice

The mammoths that first arrived in Europe about 2.5 million years ago found a mild and welcoming climate. But over the next million years, temperatures gradually dropped and winters became longer and more severe, until Europe was in the grip of an ice age. The mammoths from Africa were also adapting to the changing climate, evolving into thick-coated woolly animals that could survive on the cold, windswept plains.

No Pleistocene animals, not even hardy giants like woolly mammoths and woolly rhinoceroses, lived right on the ice sheets. Instead, they lived in areas just to the south of them, on plains that were something like today's subarctic tundra, but with many more plants to eat.

WHAT CAUSES AN ICE AGE?

The causes of ice ages are complicated and still not completely understood by scientists today. But we do know that changes in the way the earth orbits around the sun play an important role. Over a cycle of about 100,000 years, the path of the earth's orbit changes so that one hemisphere receives less sunlight than the other and becomes colder in winter. The earth also "wobbles" on its axis, so that parts of the planet may sometimes be tilted farther away from the sun. Winter ice and snow may form a blanket so thick that it doesn't completely melt, even during summer. Once ice sheets begin to cover the ground, they are likely to spread and stay for a long time. This is because glittering white ice and snow reflect most of the sun's heat back into space, rather than absorbing it as bare ground would, and the reflected sunlight has little chance to warm the earth's surface.

CROSSING CONTINENTS

During part of the Pleistocene ice age, a vast and grassy plain known as Beringia stretched from Siberia across to Alaska. So much water was frozen in ice sheets that sea levels were much lower than they are today and animals could cross from one continent to the other on dry land. And they did, in many waves of migration — bison, musk oxen, wolves, bears, sabertooth cats, and mammoths. Human beings also entered North America for the first time in the later part of this period, probably following the herds of mammoths and other game animals.

The first mammoths made the crossing about 1.5 million years ago. The descendants of these early arrivals, the Columbian mammoths, spread down into what is now the United States and even into Mexico. They were among the largest proboscideans that have ever lived, standing 13 feet (4 m) tall at the shoulder and weighing about 20,000 pounds (9,000 kg) — about as much as 130 adult human beings. Woolly mammoths arrived much later, perhaps 100,000 years ago. They lived in what is now Alaska, Canada, and the northern United States. With much sparser coats than woolly mammoths, Columbian mammoths stayed in the southern half of the continent.

(Right) Mammoths cross the land bridge known as Beringia.

(Below) This panorama shows many different Ice Age mammals in North America. The following are now extinct:

1. *the stout-legged llama,*

2. *the Columbian mammoth, descendant of the European mammoth,*

3. *the yesterday's camel,*

4. *the enormous Jefferson's ground sloth,*

5. *the western horse, native to North America, and*

6. *the sabertooth cat.*

Siberia   Beringia   Alaska

I f you started with an elephant and redesigned it for cold weather, you would end up with an animal that looked very much like a woolly mammoth. The first and most obvious design decision would be to give the animal a fur coat. A thick coat of hair covered the woolly mammoth from the tip of its tail down to its toes. A coarse outer coat had hairs up to three feet (almost 1 meter) long (**A**). Below this, next to the mammoth's skin, was a dense woolly undercoat (**B**).

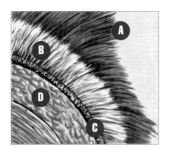

Like an elephant, a woolly mammoth had tough skin up to one inch (2.5 cm) thick (**C**). But a cold-weather elephant needs more insulation. Below the mammoth's skin was a layer of fat (**D**), four inches (10 cm) thick, to keep it warm. The woolly mammoth also had a dome on its head and a hump between its shoulders.

When designing a cold-weather animal, it is also important to consider the relationship between its surface area and its size. The more skin an animal has in relation to its size, the more body heat it loses through its skin. This is a good thing for a tropical animal but not for a northern one. Elephants, especially African elephants, have very large ear

FROM TRUNK TO TAIL

The mammoth's old, worn tooth would be pushed out by a new one growing in behind it.

flaps, which increase their surface area and help them cool off. Woolly mammoths, however, had much smaller ears to conserve body heat. They also had much shorter trunks and tails than today's elephants.

An adult mammoth had only four teeth, two in the upper jaw and two in the lower, but each one was about the size of a loaf of bread. A mammoth's diet was very hard on its teeth. We might think of grass as soft, but in fact it contains silica (a substance like glass), which grinds away the tooth's surface. And scientists estimate that a woolly mammoth munched on at least 200 pounds (90 kg) of food every day, as well as the grit that it often scooped up while eating. To cope with this wear, a mammoth grew six sets of teeth in its lifetime. As each tooth wore down to a stub, it was pushed out of the mammoth's jaw by a new one growing behind it.

A mammoth's tusks, like those of elephants today, were really just super-sized upper front teeth. They were bigger than an elephant's tusks and curved outward, then inward at the tips. The tusks grew up to six inches (15 cm) a year and kept growing throughout the animal's life, reaching total lengths of more than 13 feet (4 m). The tusks looked shorter than this in the living animal, since several feet of them were hidden inside the mammoth's skull. As they grew, new material was added to the outside of the tusks, forming rings much like the growth rings of a tree. By examining a complete cross section of a tusk, scientists can calculate a mammoth's age. The thicknesses of the rings (**E**) show stages of slower and faster growth. These would change according to the seasons, availability of food, and the state of the mammoth's health at different periods of its life.

THE VERSATILE TRUNK

Spraying Dust or Water Mammoths would use their trunks to bring water to their mouths or spray themselves.

Shoveling Snow Like its tusks, the mammoth's trunk could act as a shovel to uncover grasses beneath the snow.

A Helping Hand The mammoth had two fingerlike projections on the end of its trunk, allowing it to pick up or hold small objects. Its trunk could be used to grasp clumps of vegetation or to reach for foliage in out-of-the-way places.

FAMILY TIES

Mammoths were born and raised in herds. If they were females, they remained with the herd their entire lives. An old, wise female led the herd, drawing on a lifetime of knowledge about where to find food and water and how to avoid danger. As they grazed in the safety of the herd, mammoths had little to fear from other animals. Even a sabertooth cat would not attack a healthy adult mammoth, only the young or the sick. When males reached puberty, they went off on their own or joined casual bands of other young males. But they returned to the herd to find mates and perhaps for other kinds of reunions or for migrations.

The matriarch leads the herd in defending one of its young from a pack of sabertooth cats.

(Above) Scientists examine Columbian mammoth skeletons at the Hot Springs Mammoth Site in South Dakota.

How do we know all this about an animal that died out before any written records were kept? Scientists have learned about mammoth behavior in two ways. They have looked at the behavior of elephants in the wild and thought that mammoths — closely related to living elephants — would have acted in much the same way. But they have also studied the clues left behind by the mammoths themselves. Even bare bones can tell a dramatic story when examined by the right pair of eyes.

Mammoth bones are sometimes found in clusters — perhaps because a group of animals was killed suddenly by a flash flood or landslide. When scientists analyzed the remains of 19 adult mammoths found together in 1988 in Sevsk, Russia, 17 of them were female. They believe this was a herd much like an elephant herd today. On the other hand, at the Hot Springs Mammoth Site in South Dakota, individual mammoths accidentally fell into a sinkhole and died there over a long period of time. All except one of the skeletons found were male. Scientists believe these were young males roving away from the herd.

TUSK TALES

Mammoth tusks usually show scratches and other signs of wear on the underside. They were probably used by the animal to root up food, sweep away snow from grasses, and scrape at ice to get fresh water. They were also powerful weapons against predators and even other mammoths.

The record of one mammoth encounter about 12,000 years ago was preserved in a remarkable way. Two young male mammoths — perhaps just playing or

perhaps competing for a mate — grappled with each other and accidentally entangled their tusks. They died in the exhausting effort to free themselves — and paleontologists found their bones with the tusks still intertwined.

Two male Columbian mammoths lock tusks in an encounter that sometimes proved fatal. (Top) A fortune in mammoth and elephant tusks stored in a London warehouse in 1922.

WHAT KILLED THE MAMMOTHS?

One day, about 10,000 years ago, the last remaining mammoth in North America died. As the mammoths vanished, so too did most of the immense mammals known as *megafauna*, including mastodons, giant sloths, and sabertooth cats. Around the same time, large animals also died out in South America, Australia, northern Europe, and Asia. What defeated these rugged creatures that had

(Above) Prehistoric hunters may have trapped mammoths in pits to kill them.
(Right) A North American spearhead dating from the time mammoths became extinct.

THE WRANGEL ISLAND SURVIVORS

Long after full-sized mammoths (below, left) had vanished, at least one group of smaller mammoths survived. They lived on Wrangel Island, off the north coast of Siberia, as recently as 3,800 years ago — when the ancient Egyptians were building their pyramids. These animals stood no more than six feet (almost 2 m) tall at the shoulder (below, right). Scientists think that they were descendants of full-sized mammoths that became stranded there as water channels opened up after the ice age. Because there were no predators on the island, a mammoth's large body was no longer necessary for protection. And because there was less food on the island than on the mainland, a smaller mammoth that ate less was more likely to survive. Over thousands of years, a race of dwarf mammoths evolved. But even these eventually died out. Ross MacPhee and his colleagues have been studying these mammoths because their remains are the "freshest" anywhere in the world. They are now examining marrow from a Wrangel Island mammoth bone, looking for a hyperdisease virus that may lurk there.

survived the ice age but disappeared when the world's climate became milder?

There are several theories about these extinctions. Perhaps mammoths were wiped out by human beings who overhunted them. Some scientists point to the fact that the animals became extinct soon after hunters armed with arrows arrived in North America. However, other scientists believe these hunters may have been too few in number to have caused mass extinctions. They point out that mammoths and humans lived together in Europe and Asia for thousands of years before the mammoths there died out.

It is natural for us to think that milder weather after the last ice age made life easier for mammoths. But perhaps it didn't. Changing climate causes changes in animals' habitats. Perhaps the mammoths' grazing lands shrank. As rainfall and temperature changed, new plants may have replaced the old — plants that were not as nourishing for mammoths. Perhaps the mammoths died of starvation.

The most recent theory has been proposed by Ross MacPhee, an American paleomammalogist (a person who studies ancient mammals). He suggests that the mammoths may have been killed by a highly contagious fatal disease — a "hyperdisease," as MacPhee calls it. This disease may have been carried by human hunters or their dogs and then infected the mammoths. That would explain why they died out so soon after human beings arrived in North America. The main problem with this theory is that no one has any idea — yet — of what this disease might have been.

CAN THE WOOLLY MAMMOTH BE CLONED?

The mightiest land mammal of the ice age may find new life in our own time. Whether the mammoths will ever live again depends on tiny strands of chemicals inside their body cells. These strands of DNA (deoxyribonucleic acid) carry the genetic code, or "blueprint," for the entire mammoth.

Scientists have already extracted DNA from the cells of living animals to produce clones. (Clones are offspring that are completely identical to the animal that provided the DNA.) In 1996, they produced Dolly the sheep. Since then, other animals — calves, goats, even a litter of piglets — have been produced through cloning. Some scientists say if they could obtain usable DNA from a mammoth, they could apply the same techniques to bring these giants back from extinction.

The practical problems are huge, however. Cloning is still an experimental process with a very low success rate. For every 100 attempts to clone an animal, only two or three offspring result. Furthermore, researchers have never been able to obtain a mammoth's complete genetic code. All mammoth finds have been too damaged or decayed to yield more than a few broken fragments of DNA. Scientists hope that the Jarkov Mammoth can be thawed slowly and carefully so that fragile DNA is not destroyed. If the Jarkov Mammoth cannot provide usable DNA, the hunt will be on for another frozen mammoth.

Cloning is not the only option scientists have considered for the Jarkov Mammoth, which is a male. If they can obtain some undamaged mammoth sperm, they could use it to fertilize the egg of a female Asian elephant. (Studies have shown that Asian elephants are closer relatives of mammoths than African elephants.) The resulting offspring would be a hybrid — part mammoth, part elephant. Over several generations, selective breeding could produce an animal that would be nearly pure mammoth. But since these hybrids, like elephants, would probably not be mature enough to have babies until they were about 20 years old, it would take a long time — perhaps almost a century — to produce a near-mammoth using this approach.

(Opposite) Dolly, the first animal to be successfully cloned. (Top) A scientist takes a sample of mammoth tissue. (Right) Someday a genetic scientist may offer treats to a cloned baby mammoth.

WELCOME TO PLEISTOCENE PARK

Suppose mammoths *could* be brought back to life. Should they be? What would their fate be in a world where elephants — their modern cousins — have almost no habitat left? One possible answer to this dilemma is to release them in Pleistocene Park.

It sounds like science fiction, but this place does exist. Its headquarters are at the Northeast Science Station, located near the town of Cherskii in a remote part of Siberia. Thousands of years ago, this area was rich grassland — a landscape that scientists call *mammoth steppe* because it was once home to so many of these giant creatures. After the last ice age ended, however, the climate warmed and more rain fell. The grasslands became sodden, covered with moss and lichen and dotted with spindly shrubs and trees.

Now an international team of scientists hopes to turn back the clock. On a 62-square-mile (160-square-km) protected area, they have established Pleistocene Park. The first step of their project is already

An imaginary scene in Pleistocene Park of the future, where mammoths may live with other ice age descendants, including wood bison, Yakutian ponies, reindeer, and the Siberian tiger.

(Above) Scientists believe mammoths would greet each other by touching their trunks like elephants. (Left) The landscape of Pleistocene Park today.

well under way. In 1989, a herd of hardy Yakutian ponies — the closest descendants of the Pleistocene horses that once lived here — were introduced to the preserve. They are able to eat the scrub growth, and at the same time, their hooves are churning up the ground and keeping the moss from returning so that grasses can grow. Now the scientists are planning to add a herd of Canadian wood bison — the closest living relatives of the bison which once lived in Siberia thousands of years ago. The wood bison can feed on the grass that is now growing, and their droppings can provide rich fertilizer. Like those of the ponies, their large hooves can also churn up the ground and prevent the growth of moss. These animals will live alongside the moose and reindeer that already make their home here.

When the herds of ponies and wood bison are large and healthy, the scientists hope to add predators, perhaps even the endangered Siberian tiger, to create a true balanced ecosystem — a new mammoth steppe. And then, who knows? Perhaps one day in the future, a carefully cloned and bred woolly mammoth will throw back its head and trumpet in the Siberian air as its ancestors did so long ago.

GLOSSARY

CAT scan: An image made using a computerized-axial-tomography scan, which produces cross-sectional X-rays of a body.

DNA: Short form for deoxyribonucleic acid, a complex chemical compound found in cells and viruses that carries hereditary information.

genetic code: A series of chemical links that determine the structural and other characteristics of an organism.

habitat: The place or environment where a plant or animal normally grows or lives.

hybrid: The animal or plant offspring of two different varieties or strains.

lichen: A low-growing plant, usually green, grey or yellow, found on rocks and trunks of trees.

mammals: Warm-blooded animals with fur or hair that nourish their young with milk.

mammoth steppe: A level, grassy, unforested plain in Europe and Siberia that once supported herds of mammoths.

matriarch: The female leader of a group or family.

megafauna: The group of large mammals, usually 100 pounds (44 kg) or bigger, which are now extinct.

paleontologist: A scientist who studies the remains of extinct plants or animals.

parasite: An organism living on or in another creature and depending on it for its existence, often to the disadvantage of the host.

Pleistocene Epoch: The period from approximately 1.7 million to 10,000 years ago, marked by great changes in temperature and sheets of ice advancing and retreating.

predator: A creature that hunts and kills another for food.

selective breeding: When humans manipulate the inherited characteristics of animal or plant offspring.

sinkhole: A large circular depression in the ground formed by water dissolving soil beneath it or by the collapse of an underground cave.

subarctic tundra: A treeless plain covered in moss, lichen, and low shrubs, found just outside the arctic region.

vertebrae: Plural form of *vertebra*, one of the bony segments forming the spine.

RECOMMENDED FURTHER READING

Mammoth: Ice Age Bones and Book
by Barbara Hehner, Somerville House
A lively and informative small-format book that comes with a build-your-own mammoth skeleton kit.

Mammoths by Adrian Lister and Paul Bahn, Macmillan U.S.A.
This is *the* comprehensive reference book on mammoths, complete with numerous illustrations, photographs, diagrams, and maps of major mammoth finds in the world.

Wild and Woolly Mammoths
by Aliki, HarperCollins
This beautifully illustrated book for younger readers has recently been revised and updated.

WEB SITES

www.beringia.com/index.html The Yukon Beringia Interpretive Centre's web site presents information about the story of Beringia and the animals that once lived there.

www.discovery.com/exp/mammoth/mammoth.html The Discovery Channel's web site featuring the expedition to excavate the Jarkov Mammoth. Fascinating photographs, updates on the latest discoveries, and all sorts of information, including interactive quizzes and games.

www.mammothsite.com The Mammoth Site of Hot Springs, South Dakota, gives a virtual tour of the museum and plenty of information about this treasure trove of Columbian mammoth remains.

www.school.discovery.com/schooladventures/woollymammoth/index.html Play "Seven Steppes to A Woollier Mammoth" and follow the Mammoth Migration Map at this informative site.

PICTURE CREDITS

All illustrations are by Mark Hallett unless otherwise stated.
2, 4: Reuters NewMedia Inc./CORBIS
5: (Top) Reuters NewMedia Inc./CORBIS; (bottom) AFP Agence France Presse, Paris/ISI
7: (Top) Bettmann/CORBIS; (bottom) Science Photo Picture Library/ISI
8: C.M. Dixon
9: (Left) C.M. Dixon; (top right) Dean Conger/CORBIS/ISI, (bottom right) Science Photo Picture Library/ISI
15, 17: Maps by Jack McMaster
22: Jonathan Blair/CORBIS
23: Bettmann/CORBIS
24: Aldo Tutino, Art Resource, NY
26, 27: Science Photo Picture Library/ISI
30: Courtesy Sergei Zimov

INDEX

ACKNOWLEDGMENTS

With thanks to my editor, Susan Aihoshi, for her special care with this project. — *Barbara Hehner*

I would like to credit the inspiration and encouragement given to me as a child in drawing mammoths by my aunt, Merlyn McLean. She made sure I was able to see these when we visited the Field Museum in Chicago many years ago, and her love and enthusiasm for nature has always made a great impression on me. — *Mark Hallett*

Madison Press Books would like to thank the following individuals for their invaluable assistance: our scientific consultants, Dr. Mark Engstrom, director of research and senior curator of mammals in the Centre for Biodiversity and Conservation Biology at the Royal Ontario Museum, and Dr. Kevin Seymour, assistant curator of Paleobiology at the Royal Ontario Museum; Melissa Chapin of the Institute of Arctic Biology, University of Alaska, Fairbanks, and Sergei Zimov of the Northeast Science Station in Cherskii, Siberia.

Text, design, and compilation
© 2001 The Madison Press Limited
Illustrations © 2001 Mark Hallett

First published by
Crown Publishers, a division of Random House, Inc.
1540 Broadway, New York, New York 10036

CROWN and colophon are trademarks of Random House, Inc.

www.randomhouse.com/kids

Library of Congress Cataloging-in-Publication Data

Hehner, Barbara.
Ice Age mammoth: will this ancient giant come back to life? / Barbara Hehner; illustrated by Mark Hallett. — 1st ed.
p.   cm.
Includes bibliographical references and index.
1. Woolly mammoth—Juvenile literature.
[1. Woolly mammoth. 2. Mammoths.
3. Prehistoric animals.]
I. Hallett, Mark, 1947– , ill. II. Title.
QE882.P8 H43   2001
569'.67—dc21   00-066023

ISBN 0-375-81327-6 (trade) —
ISBN 0-375-91327-0 (lib. bdg.)

Printed in Belgium

October 2001
10 9 8 7 6 5 4 3 2 1

Editorial Director: Hugh Brewster
Project Editor: Susan Aihoshi
Editorial Assistance: Joanne Chow,
    Lloyd Davis, Ingrid Mida,
    Wanda Nowakowska, Imoinda Romain
Book Design: Gordon Sibley Design Inc.
Maps and Diagrams: Jack McMaster
Picture Research: Image Select
    International Ltd.
Production Director: Susan Barrable
Production Manager: Donna Chong
Color Separation: Colour Technologies
Printing and Binding: Proost
    International, Belgium

ICE AGE MAMMOTH
was produced by Madison Press Books, which is under the direction of Albert E. Cummings

Produced by
Madison Press Books
1000 Yonge Street
Toronto, Ontario, Canada
M4W 2K2